Green Animals

by Teddy Borth

ABDO
ANIMAL COLORS
Kids

abdopublishing.com

Published by Abdo Kids, a division of ABDO, PO Box 398166, Minneapolis, Minnesota 55439.

Copyright © 2015 by Abdo Consulting Group, Inc. International copyrights reserved in all countries. No part of this book may be reproduced in any form without written permission from the publisher.

Printed in the United States of America, North Mankato, Minnesota.

102014

012015

THIS BOOK CONTAINS
RECYCLED MATERIALS

Photo Credits: iStock, Minden Pictures, Shutterstock, Thinkstock, © Nicholas Curtis and Ray Martinez p.20

Production Contributors: Teddy Borth, Jennie Forsberg, Grace Hansen

Design Contributors: Candice Keimig, Laura Rask, Dorothy Toth

Library of Congress Control Number: 2014943665

Cataloging-in-Publication Data

Borth, Teddy.

 Green animals / Teddy Borth.

   p. cm. -- (Animal colors)

ISBN 978-1-62970-695-5 (lib. bdg.)

Includes index.

1. Animals--Juvenile literature.   I. Title.

590--dc23

                    2014943665

Table of Contents

Green

Green is a **secondary color**.
Painters make green by
mixing yellow and blue.

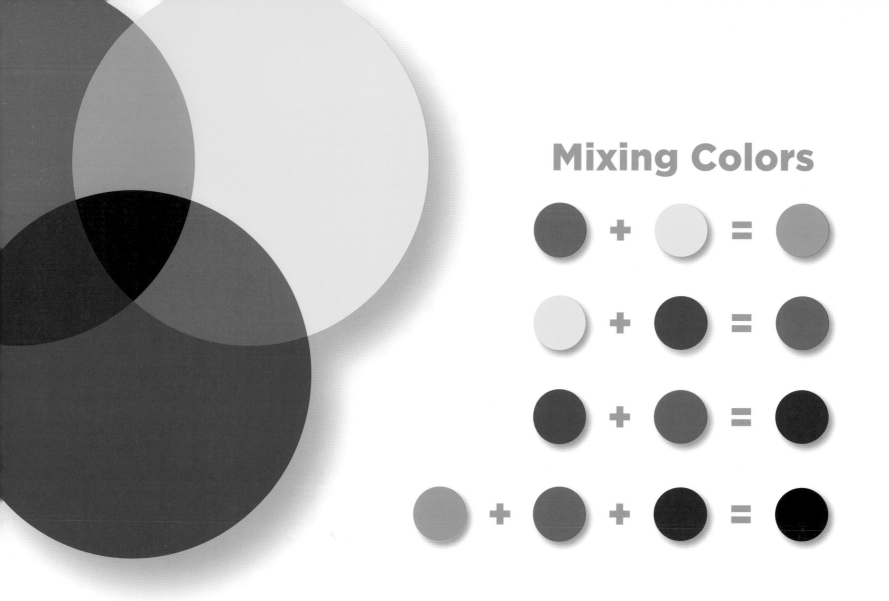

Mixing Colors

Primary Colors

- Red
- Yellow
- Blue

Secondary Colors

- Orange
- Green
- Purple

5

Green on Land

The tree python is green.
It sleeps in trees. It makes
a bed with its body.

European tree frogs are green. They **croak** when rain is coming. People use tree frogs as a weather report.

Tree sloths move slowly.

Algae grows on them.

This turns their fur green.

The green basilisk lives in the rain forest. It can run across water. It can stay under water for 30 minutes.

13

Many caterpillars are green. They will become butterflies or moths.

Green in Air

Amazon parrots have green feathers. They are popular pets. They can repeat words.

There are 2,400 kinds
of mantis. The praying
mantis uses green to
hide. It can look like a leaf.

19

Green in Water

Green sea slugs eat **algae**.

This makes them green.

They get energy from

the sun like a plant.

20

More Facts

- Most green animals use green to hide and be safe.

- Green is known as a safe color. Traffic lights, train signals, and ship signals all use green to mean "go."

- Green is the color of spring, growth, nature, youth, hope, greed, and envy.

22

Glossary

algae – simple plants that grow in water.

croak – a deep sound made by a frog.

envy – to want what somebody else has.

greed – wanting more than one needs.

primary color – a color that cannot be made by mixing other colors.

secondary color – a color resulting from mixing two primary colors.

Index

abdokids.com

Use this code to log on to abdokids.com and access crafts, games, videos, and more!

Abdo Kids Code:
AGK6955